ART SHOW BASICS

Modern Artist's Handbook Vol 3

A How-To Template For Putting On An Art Show

Gail Daley

GAIL DALEY

ART SHOW BASICS – MODERN ARTIST'S HANDBOOK VOL 3

ACKNOWLEDGEMENT

I would like to thank the Clovis Art Guild of Clovis California for the use of their forms as examples in this work. The Art Guild is a regional association devoted to the encouragement and education of the visual arts on local levels.

ART SHOW BASICS – MODERN ARTIST'S HANDBOOK VOL 3

DISCLAIMER

Disclaimer: The information in this booklet is for general information purposes only; it is not intended to be tax or legal advice. Each situation is specific; consult your CPA or attorney to discuss your specific legal or tax requirements or questions.

ART SHOW BASICS – MODERN ARTIST'S HANDBOOK VOL 3

COPYRIGHT

ART SHOW BASICS – MODERN ARTIST'S HANDBOOK VOL 3

Table of Contents

OVERVIEW OF AN ART SHOW

Whether you are organizing a group show, or having a one-man show or exhibit, don't be fooled: there is a lot of work connected with an art show. You must decide where and when you are going to hold the show and how much are you going to spend. If it is a group show, you will need to decide if it is going to be judged or if you are simply putting on an exhibit. If you are doing a solo or one-man show for yourself, then these decisions are going to be up to you. If you are organizing a group show, there probably will be others who will have a say in these items.

With a group show, you should be prepared to delegate responsibilities if possible. Some of the things you may be able to delegate:

- Making the Prospectus, Show Catalogs and display cards
- Publicity
- Decorating the Show room
- Catering the reception

Budget: It is best to know ahead of time how much you will need to cover expenses, so a budget is a must. If you have no idea how much some of these things are going to cost, then you need the advice of someone who has experience in organizing a show. In an art association, the groups Treasurer will be a good resource for this.

SHOW BUDGET

Here is a list of budget items

Budget $____			Ordered?	Dollar amt	Pick-up Date
Location					
	Deposit				
	Rental				
	Parking				
Judges Fee					
Advertising/Publicity					
Show Catalogs					
	Identifying cards for art				
Ribbons & Trophies					
Awards					
Reception					
	Food				
	Decoration			0	

Location: Finding a location is your first order of business. You need a site that is large enough to hold the art and will be open during the show hours. Preferably it should be in an area with a lot of walk-in traffic and easily accessible to the public.

QUESTIONS TO ASK THE VENUE:

- is there a deposit or rental fee?
- Does the venue require the show to be open during certain hours?
- How secure will the art be?
- Does the show require an attendant when it is open?
- Is there a commission on sales?

(It is always best to "sit" the show, unless it is not accessible to walk-in traffic. This will prevent theft or damage to the art.) In real estate, the words *"location, location, location"* are very popular. These are popular words in art shows as well. *A successful show must be seen by the public.* A location where there is a high volume of foot traffic and visited by a lot of art fans is ideal. A location such as this may be pricey, but if an audience is already there and primed to visit the show, you won't need to spend as much on advertising to drive buyers to see it. If possible, find out what venues the group has used in the past and check them out. If you can get opinions from other art groups who have used the venue, this is also valuable in deciding on a site.

Deposit: Almost all venues that you rent are going to require a percentage of the rental fee as a deposit. Find out how much this is up front. It may or may not be refundable if you or the venue changes your mind, so get this in writing as a part of your rental contract.

Rental: How much are you willing to spend to rent the space? You will need to weigh the cost of the space against how much you expect to make on sales. (This is true even if you are taking part in an outdoor show where you are renting booth space.)

How to Display: If the venue has a hanging system already in place, you only need to ensure that any art coming in is compatible with their system. If they don't have a system, then you will need to find out how they expect you to display the art. Will they let you put up screws or sticky holders on the wall? If whatever you use damages their wall, who does the repair? And what kind of repair will they expect? Unless your art is very heavy (more that 15 lbs.) I recommend those removable sticky holders to hang your art on walls rather than screws or nails. Two or three per art piece will spread out the weight of a painting, they have a lip to hang wires, and usually the stickers will come right off and you won't have to spend a lot of money on spackle and paint to repair the wall.

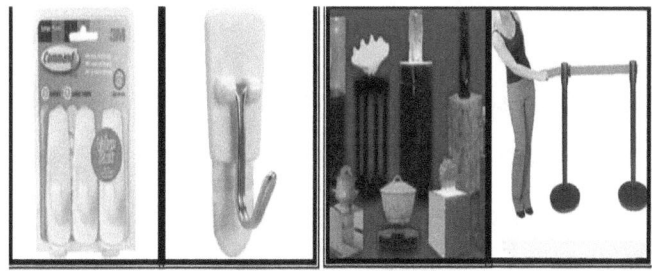

If you are displaying sculpture, there are other considerations: is the sculpture reachable by the public? Does it have sharp edges? Is it small enough to develop legs and walk out? For larger sculptures, I recommend a system of ropes to keep the public away from the art piece. Check with the venue to see if they have some. If they don't, you will either should take your chances that someone gets hurt or damages the art. DO NOT set up a jury-rigged affair if you want your display to look professional. For the smaller sculptures, I recommend a pedestal with a plexi cover and placing it either against the wall or in an area where it isn't likely to be bumped.

Parking: unless your show is in an area where potential buyers customarily walk to visit art galleries, you will need to make sure that easily accessible, low-cost parking is available to your show. Easy access by the public includes parking (preferably free parking). A venue may offer you a great deal, but if no one comes to see the show than the show can't be said to be successful.

LIABILITY INSURANCE

insurance questions cannot be answered by anyone other than your insurance carrier. At a minimum, you should have theft and personal liability coverage. Only your insurance agent can tell you what your state requires or recommends. The venue may also have requirements for coverage and they may want a rider from your company naming them as an additional insured for the show. Whatever their requirements are—***get it in writing!*** Art associations usually have an insurance carrier with liability coverage for shows. If you are doing a group show, ask the group treasurer to make sure that the group's insurance amount meets the venue's coverage requirements.

SELECTING A JUDGE

If this is a juried group show, then most probably the group will already have a judge's fee schedule in place and will decide as a group who the judge is going to be but some groups prefer the show coordinator to at least present a list of likely candidates. If you are the show coordinator and don't have a list of judges to draw from, then ask the group if they have one. The best person to co-ordinate with on judging will be the person who arranges art demonstrations for the group. You can also check around the local art community for art teachers with a highly-respected reputation.

When the judge arrives at the show, there are basic instructions to be given, and these instructions will need to be agreed upon by the art group in your preliminary show discussions.

- Can the Best of Show be taken from any category regardless of any rules concerning the number of pieces required for a category to be judged?
- Can Best of Show be chosen before judging any categories?
- How many pieces of art you can hang?
- How much culling you expect the judge to do?
- Should the judge offer on-going critiques as he or she judges?

If this is the case, you will need a volunteer to take notes. If you have multiple judges, you need to instruct those judges as to how they come to an agreement if they differ on the rating of an art piece. FYI: With multiple judges if you don't want a lot of negotiating about awarding the prizes among the judges, it is better for them to use silent score sheets with ratings for sections to judge the items. Any differences in rating can then be negotiated among the judges verbally. This will cut down on the amount of time it takes to judge a show. Whether to use score sheets with multiple judges is usually a matter for the group to decide. An example is included in the sample section.

ADVERTISING/PUBLICITY

How much can you afford to spend on this? A lot of TV and radio stations offer Community Affairs sites where you can unload information concerning your event, reception, sale, etc for free. It helps if you are promoting Charity as well (10% of your sales will go to something like Valley Children's Hospital, or the SPCA, etc.). These advertising spots will probably run during "public service" times. Prime advertising times in most traditional methods of advertising will require hard cash up front. Bear in mind that these media outlets aren't interested in an event that has already taken place. Advertise an upcoming reception or award ceremony ahead of time. Some of the traditional media outlets have time frame deadlines of several weeks ahead that need to be met to get an article printed. **If you are doing a group show for an organization, you may be able to turn this portion of the show to the group's publicity chairman.**

SHOW PROSPECTUS

A prospectus is a fancy word for an entry form for the show. The more eye-catching and colorful it looks, the more the artists you are trying to attract as entrants will notice it. It should have the following information: location, date and time of receiving for the show; length of the show and the date, time and location to pick up the art after the show; the date of the artist reception; Entry fees and the number of art pieces per artist allowed. It should also contain a section called *The Rules of Exhibit* carrying information concerning the categories of the art permitted in the show, what type of items are NOT allowed and hanging requirements. A fill-in section for each art piece is usually included, along with a cut-off portion for an artist receipt to be presented at the close of the show to pick up the art.

If this is an annual show, a copy of the new prospectus should be mailed out to last year's entrants. The prospectus should be as widely distributed as possible. Once dates and times are locked down, making the prospectus can usually be designated to a member of the group with the graphic skills to make it. A sample is included in the Sample section.

SAMPLE TRI-FOLD

PROSPECTUS

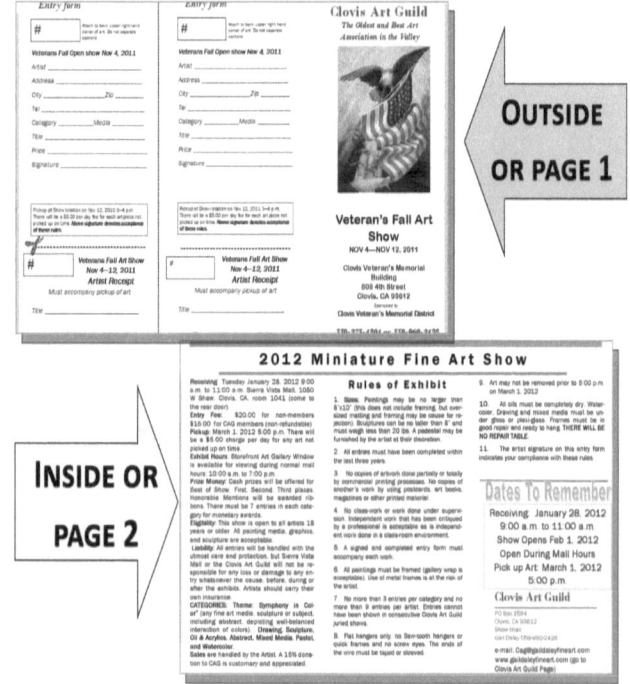

RECEIVING

For receiving you will need the following personnel:

The Treasurer there to take entry fees
  and write receipts.

An artist experienced in shows to examine each art piece as it comes in to ensure that it meets the show requirements as to framing and hanging. You may or may not choose to have a repair table for artists whose art doesn't meet the requirements to make on-the-spot repairs. If you do, you should charge a fee for the materials and advice.

One person per show category to log in
  the artwork in each category.

I recommend a secondary log-in system on a tablet or laptop. Whoever is making the catalog can copy and past information from these logs to create the show catalog. This will save time and error as it creates a second look at each entry. You will also need Log in Sheets for each entry category.

Volunteers or "Runners": You will also need volunteers to assist in bringing in art for the judge to see and taking it back. It is important that you instruct these volunteers in the conduct expected of them. Yes, even those volunteers who have assisted before. "Runners" to handle the art. Runners are volunteers who receive the art from the artist after it has been logged in and then put it with other art in that category. In this way, the art has already been collected and sorted into the proper categories when it comes time to present it to the judge. A few simple rules to give the volunteers to follow:

- no talking while the judge is working (judging a category).
- Don't offer opinions unless asked and
- don't second-guess the judge among yourselves during judging (especially out loud).
- If anyone has issues with winners chosen by the judge, they should express them privately.

SAMPLE SHOW LOG IN

SHEET

Award	#	Artist Name	Address	Phone no	title	Media	Price
	201						
	202						
	203						
	204						
	205						
	206						
	207						
	208						
	209						

SHOW CATALOGS

A show catalog serves two purposes 1) it identifies each piece of art and hopefully also shows the price of that art and instructions as to how to buy it. 2) If a prospective buyer takes it home with them, it can also be a resource for viewers to consider if they decide to buy a piece of art from the show.

Your catalog should appear professional. A catalog can be a trifold brochure or a booklet, depending on the amount of information it needs to hold. A price list **_tacked to the window or wall won't cut it._** If this is a group show, then find out who usually makes their show catalogs and coordinate with that person.

Exactly what should appear in a show catalog? Each piece of art should be clearly identified by show item number, title of the art, price, artist's name and media to match the card placed beside each art piece. A nice cover page announcing the duration and hours of the show, information about the judge and a section on how to purchase the art must be included. If the group has sold advertising to help defray the price of printing the catalog, then those items are usually located in the rear of the catalog. If this is a one-man show, then usually a simple color trifold brochure with your contact information will look good. If you have the skills to make it yourself, save money by doing so. You may find when it comes to printing it however that it is cheaper to take the design to a printer like Kinkos or Impress to print rather than spend a lot of money on colored ink to print it yourself. Remember this cost must be included in your budget. There are samples at the end of the book.

SAMPLE SHOW CATALOG – MULTI ARTIST SHOW

Your catalog should appear professional. A catalog can be a trifold brochure or a booklet, depending on the amount of information it needs to hold. Here is a partial representation of the front of a trifold catalog brochure. Although catalogs and prospectus can be built in word or pages, a good publisher program is invaluable in this for this sort of thing.

101 Art Title   ›$
        Artist   Media

To Inquire about purchasing art in this show
please talk to the show host/hostess

*NSF means "NOT FOR SALE" but you may
contact the artist concerning prints

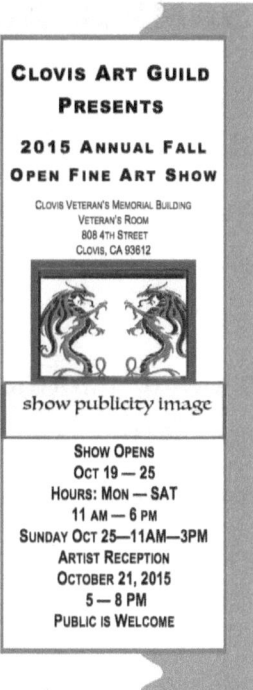

CLOVIS ART GUILD
PRESENTS

2015 ANNUAL FALL
OPEN FINE ART SHOW

CLOVIS VETERAN'S MEMORIAL BUILDING
VETERAN'S ROOM
808 4TH STREET
CLOVIS, CA 93612

show publicity image

SHOW OPENS
OCT 19 — 25
HOURS: MON — SAT
11 AM — 6 PM
SUNDAY OCT 25—11AM—3PM
ARTIST RECEPTION
OCTOBER 21, 2015
5 — 8 PM
PUBLIC IS WELCOME

SAMPLE ART SHOW ID TAG

All shows should have identifying cards for every art piece matching the information on the catalog. These should be placed next to each art piece and have the following information: show item number, title of the art, price, artist's name and media. Cards should be typed or hand printed by someone with VERY good printing skills.

The size of the ID card may vary. The most common sizes are 3 x 5 or business card size. FYI: DO NOT stick your business card with the name of the painting and the price scrawled on it next to your art! It looks tacky and unprofessional!

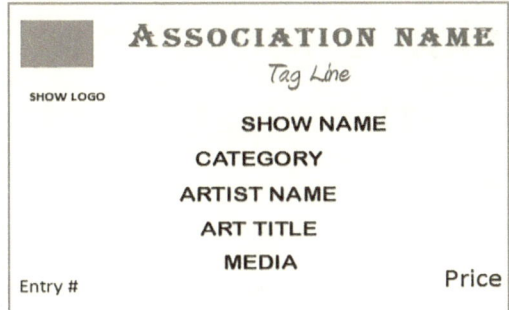

AWARDS, RIBBONS & TROPHIES

How much is going to be spent for awards, ribbons & trophies if this is a group show? Most places that make ribbons and trophies charge more for a small "run" than they do for a large one. If possible use only the group name on each ribbon, and avoid putting the year, or if the group does more than one show per year, a title for the show. In this way, leftover ribbons can be used at a later show. The group's treasurer can tell you who the group orders ribbons from and place the order. Ribbons are generally given for Best of Show, 1st, 2nd, 3rd and honorable mentions in each category. Sometimes a yellow ribbon is also given for "People's Choice" (visitors to the show can vote on their favorite art piece). You will need to coordinate with the groups Treasurer to find out where these items are usually ordered.

Cash awards for Best of Show, 1st, 2nd and 3rd amounts are usually arrived at by using a percentage of the show entries and may vary from show to show. Sponsors may also donate items in kind also as a portion of the show awards. Some shows require that there be a certain number of entries in a category for money to be awarded.

RECEPTION

Sometimes the venue will decide when to hold the artist reception. If this is the case, there is a schedule in the sample section to help you keep track of expenses. If you or the group are handling refreshments for the reception, then the main issue when scheduling is making sure it is held at a time that the most people will be able to attend.

Food: keep it simple. The patrons are there to see at the art, not eat. If the group is supplying the food, then coordinate with their food chairman as to type and amount of food. Special decorations for the food tables should be left up to him or her if possible, but if items need to be purchased, then this is a budget item. If the reception is catered, then the same rules apply, but more money will probably be needed.

Seating: small groups (no more than 2 or 3) of artistically placed chairs so patrons can sit and study the art is always nice.

Decoration: while you want the venue to appear well-put together, decorations should not overshadow the art. A few tablecloths on the tables, flower vases, draping the chairs for seating to look less utilitarian, etc. is all that is needed.

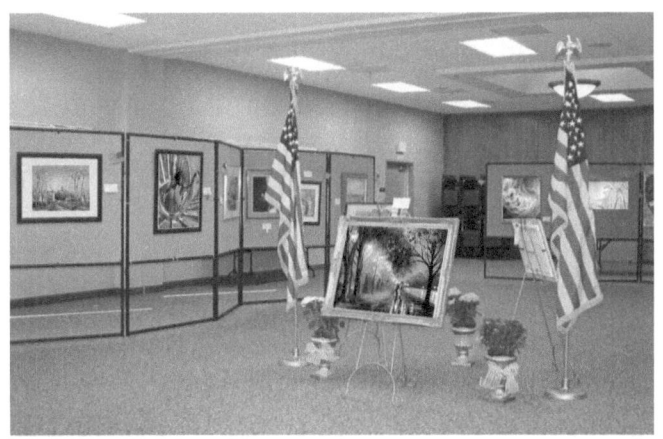

SHOW DÉCOR

Always have an information table with information about the group (or about you if you if it is a one-man show). A guest book to add interested guests to your mailing list should be on the information table. Make sure your host or hostess knows to ask them to sign up for future notifications. Show catalogs are essential.

A show host or hostess to make sure that guests have information and a catalog when they enter is always nice. If you are doing a one-man show, try to arrange for someone else to act as host or hostess so that you are free to mingle and make contacts with the guests.

While sales may take place at the reception, be sure buyers know that the art needs to stay up for the duration of the show. Most shows elect to have the individual artists handle their own sales and simply collect a 20% is customary commission on the sale from the artist. With non-profit art associations, this payment is voluntary on the part of the artist.

A show profit/loss statement is included in the samples at the end of the booklet which should be prepared with the Treasurers assistance after the show. If you are lucky, the Treasurer will do the entire thing for you since he/she will be collecting the money and writing the checks.

SAMPLE SHOW REPORT

Expenses			Income		No of Entries Needed to break even		
Judge		$150.00	Entry Fees	$0.00	Entry Fees $20/	70	
Awards based on 8 categories			Grants	$0.00	Entry fee $15/	94	
	Best of Show	$150.00	Commissions	$0.00	Entry fees $10/	141	
	1st Places - $50 ea	$400.00		$0.00			
	2nd Places - $25 ea	$200.00		$0.00			
	3rd Places - $15 ea	$120.00		$0.00			
Advertising		$200.00		$0.00			
Ribbons		$45.00		$0.00			
sub total		$1,265.00		$0.00			
Postage		$50.00		$0.00			
Printing				$0.00			
	Prospectus	$65.00		$0.00			
	show catalog	$25.00		$0.00			
		$90.00		$0.00			
				$0.00			
Total Expenses		$1,405.00	Total Income	$0.00		net profit/ loss	

THE OBJECT OF AN ART SHOW

Art shows come in many types and are subject to various factors (themes, venue size etc.) there are some basic principles to making sure the art displayed is pleasing to the eye. Art shows do two things: showcase art and (hopefully) sell the art. If something is out of kilter, the viewer will subconsciously be Ill at ease when looking at the show. This will make everyone who sees it much less likely to buy a print or painting.

TYPES OF SHOWS

Art shows have two basic types to consider when hanging: A show where all the art is the same size and framed the same way. This is usually done with a photography show, or a solo show by a single artist. The other type of show has art received in all shapes, medias and sizes from many artists. This is usually a competitive art show of some type. Hanging this type of show can be a challenge. The first thing to consider is where the art is to be hung; i.e. on a wall or on art standards. While the principles of hanging are the same, how the effects are achieved is very different.

HANGING GROUPS TOGEHER VS SEPARATELY

Most art shows are organized either by subject matter or by media type. It is tempting to group all the florals together, or all the landscapes, animals, etc., but this is not a good idea. The human eye is a funny thing. When viewing the same types of images for very long it gets tired.

Studies have shown that when looking at as few as three of the same type of images for any length of time details are lost and it becomes more difficult to remember individual images. The object of an art show is to allow each artist who entered the opportunity for their art piece to have maximum impact. To keep the viewers eye from becoming tired, it is important to vary both the subject matter and color palette of each art piece when setting up the show. If it is at all possible, hang art with different subject matter and media close to each other. For maximum impact on the viewer, hang a landscape next to a floral or a portrait or vice versa. If it isn't possible, to do this (landscapes or a subject, may outnumber all the other art for instance) then consider hanging different medias together, say hang a watercolor next to an oil. Even if both happen to have the same subject, both seascapes for instance, the look a feel of a delicate watercolor will be very different from a vibrant oil painting, so a viewer's eye won't think it is seeing the same image over and over.

Many artists today buy their frames in standard sizes from the on-line sellers so it is possible that different artists will submit art in frames looking exactly alike. Hanging the art together will increase the chance the viewer may consider them a "set". There are two views about this: one idea says that this increases the chance of selling both pieces; the other school of thought feels this can decrease the impact of each individual piece.

THE SAME SIZE ART

This is a show where all the art is framed exactly alike and is the same size. This usually occurs in a solo show or in photography shows, but it can happen if a paint artist has a series of paintings all the same size and in identical frames.

As you can see in **EXAMPLE 1,** every piece of art is the same height and the same distance apart. If it is necessary to drag out a ruler and measuring tape to ensure this, then do it. Hanging the art in this manner prevents the show from looking sloppy, and if there is one piece of art the artist wants highlighted, putting it at a different level or making it a different size will give it more emphasis.

EXAMPLE 2 shows second way to hang a show so it appears pleasing to the eye by staggering the art. In this method, every other piece is hung the same height and the same distance apart from each other.

Be warned: If your measurements are off, the viewer's eye will be uneasy; it is human nature to enjoy looking at harmony. If something is out of kilter, the viewer will subconsciously be Ill at ease when looking at the show. This will make whoever sees it much less likely to buy a print or painting.

**EXAMPLE
1**

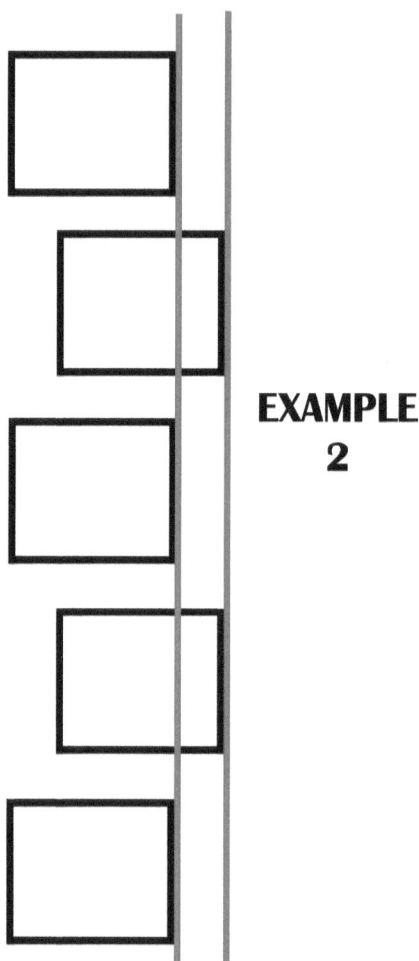

**EXAMPLE
2**

3 DIFFERENT SIZED ART PIECES

The next example is how to hang 3 differently sized pieces of art on the same standard. Instead of measuring from the outside in, start with the center line. In this case, the top of art 2 and the bottom of art 3 are approximately the same distance from the top and bottom of art 1. Art 2 and Art 3 share the center line. Because the art is differently sized, whoever hangs it can get away with a small fudge factor in the distance from the sides of the standard.

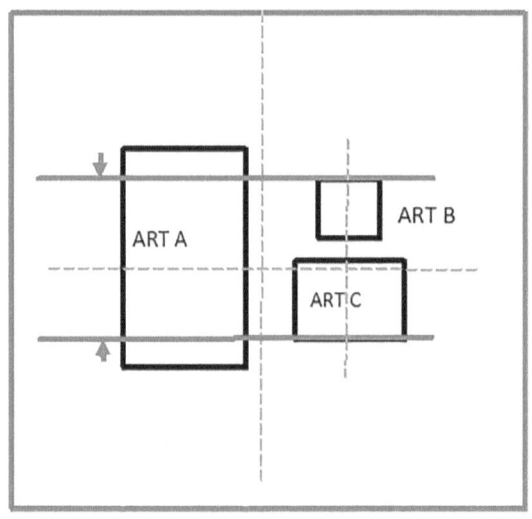

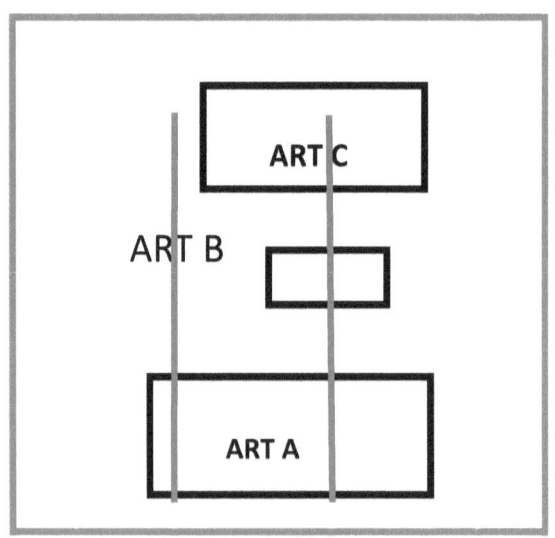

ONE LARGE ART PIECE

This is a fine example of a single large piece of large art hung on a standard. Please note that the top, bottom and sides are equidistant from the edges of the standard. If there is a sign that will appear with that piece art (Best of show, Judge, etc. the sign should be considered a part of the art. A single piece of art on a single standard should always appear this way. This applies no matter the size of the art or if it is square, landscape or portrait style. If the art is hung too high, or two low, the viewer's eye will unconsciously be drawn away from the art to look for something in the blank or "dead" area of the standard. When hanging portrait or landscape pieces, the top and bottom should be the same distance from the edge, and each side should be the same distance. Example: top and bottom about 12″ from the top and bottom of the standard, and each side about 15″. It's not necessary to be exact; eyeball it visually and that will be sufficient.

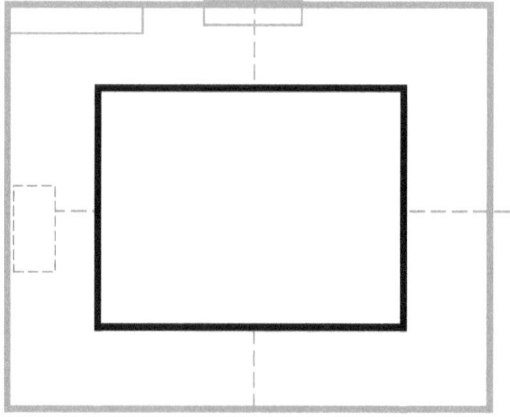

VERY TINY ART

If the art to be hung is all very small (8 x 10 or smaller) and of differing sizes, it can be difficult to hang without looking as if the space is too large for the art, giving the impression the display is "lost". Your best bet is to decide which piece of art you want as a center piece and then stager the others around it. In this case, it is all about the aligning the centers of each piece of art to create a harmonious whole. The outside pieces should also be roughly equidistant from each other

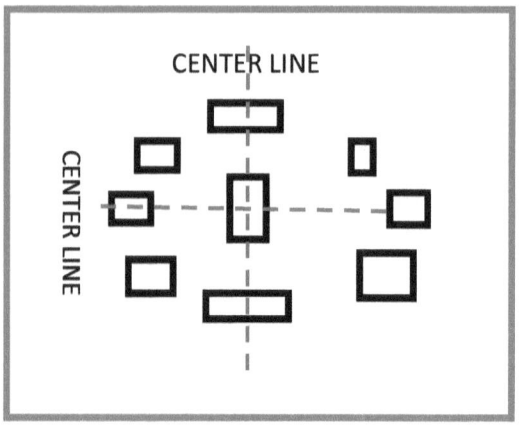

TWO SAME-SIZE PIECES

Art canvas comes in standard sizes, so it happens that occasionally several artists will submit the same size pieces of art. This is only an issue if the artists also used the same frame. Hanging the art side by side will create the impression they are a "pair", shrinking the impact of each individual piece. One of the ways to avoid this is to stagger the pieces. As with hanging the three-piece set discussed earlier, start with the center line. Art A should be hung roughly equidistant from the top and bottom of the standards. Art B needs to be placed so the top of the art is about 1/3 from the top of Art A. The distance between the two pieces (depending on their size) should be between 1/2 and 1/4 of the narrowest part of the art. Avoid hanging the art right on the edge of the standard or the display will look crowded. The line from the top and bottom of the standard creates a distraction. Hanging too close to the edge of the standard is the equalivent of having a big straight line running off the edge of your art. A minimum of two to three inches from the edge is suggested. This is true whether Landscape or portrait oriented art is being hung.

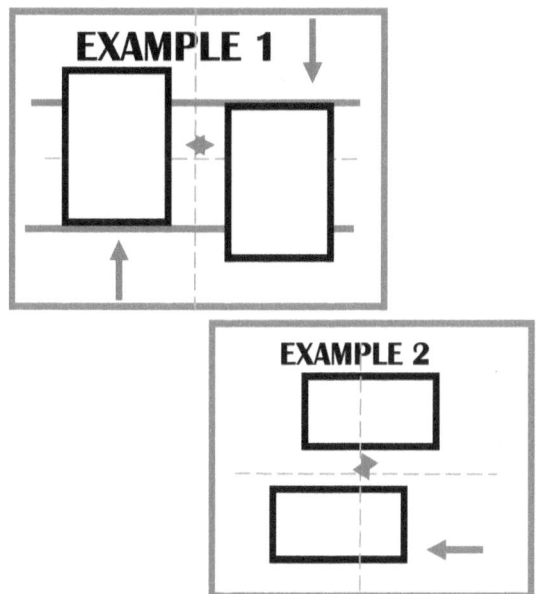

TWO DIFFERENT SIZED PIECES

While it is always best to hang art close to equal sizes together on the same standard, this is not always possible. If the larger piece is landscape oriented, it should always be placed on the bottom to avoid "overpowering" the smaller art. The center line of the small piece should line up with the center line of the larger one. The bottom edge of the larger piece should be roughly the same distance from the edge of the standard as the top edge of the smaller piece. (EXAMPLE 1)

If the larger piece is portrait oriented, the placement of the smaller piece becomes very important to its impact. Whichever side (left or right) the larger piece is placed doesn't matter. What matters is that the center line of the smaller piece be hung on the same as the Center line as the larger one. Any other placement of the smaller piece will create the impression something is missing from the standard, distracting the viewer from both art pieces. The edge side of the larger piece should be roughly the same distance from the edge of the standard as the edge side of the smaller piece from the standard. (EXAMPLE 2)

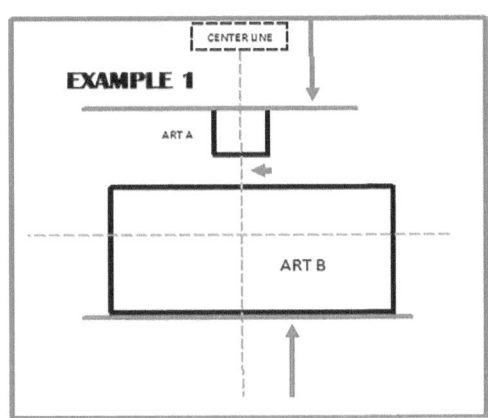

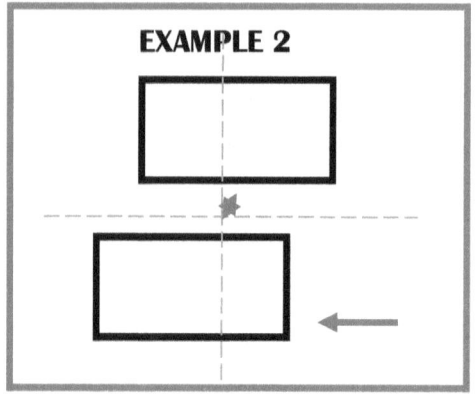

SAMPLE VENUE CONTRACT (SOLO SHOW)

This is an agreement between the artist:

_____,

whose   address   is

_____

_____, CA, _____,

hereafter known as "Artist" to hang artworks in the Venue whose address is below.

And

The   business   establishment

_____,

whose   address   is

_____

_____,

CA, _____, hereafter known as "Venue.

The term of this agreement will be for
_____, beginning on
_____ _____, 20_____.

The artist will bring art to the Venue on
the designated dates to be mutually
agreed upon with the Venue. An
inventory list of the Art will be provided
to the Venue.

HANGING ART: Art will be hung by the
artist either using a hanging system
supplied by the Venue, or by the artist
putting up screws or nails to secure the
art. If the artist puts up screws or nails,
the artist agrees to do everything
possible to minimize the damage to the
Venue's walls by making as few holes
as possible (in other words the artist
will make every effort to utilize screws
or nails already in use when changing
out the art).

Art must be hung within twenty-four (24)

hours of being received at the Venue Location.

The artist will supply an identifying tag alongside each piece of art identifying the artist, medium and price of the art.

Although the Venue may veto individual pieces of art as not suitable for their establishment, the artist will choose which art pieces to bring in. The artist usually finds that a variety of art (abstracts, landscapes, still Lifes, figures, animals, etc.) is visually agreeable.

SELLING THE ART: The Venue may choose to handle sales of the art for the artist, taking a twenty percent (20%) commission on the art, or allow sales to be handled by the individual artist. If the sale is handled by the artist, any employee of the Venue who facilitates a sale is eligible to receive a 3% commission from the artist. Sales should be recorded on the Art inventory list. **Please initial below which option is chosen by the Venue.**

_____ (initial) The Venue chooses to handle sales of the art and take a 20% commission from each sale. Payment to the artist is to be given within two (2) weeks of the final sale.

_____ (initial) The Venue chooses to allow all sales of art to be handled directly by each artist. The artist agrees to pay the facilitating employee the three percent (3%) commission within two (2) weeks of the final sale.

REMOVAL OF ART: Once hung, the art will remain in place except during regular change outs of the art by the artist unless sold. Unless the art is being sold to a customer, the Venue may not remove the art or take it down from the display area without three (3) days warning to the artist. The art may not be taken off the premises other than by the artist or the artist's agent.

OWNERSHIP OF THE ART: All art hung remains the property of the artist and is not to be considered an asset of the Venue in cases of closure or financial reverses. If the Venue closes for other than normal business hours, notice must be given within (3) days of closure so that the artist may remove the art.

_____ (initial) the artist will hang art on _____ _____, 20____.

_____

Date ____/____/_____

The artist

_____ ___

Date __/____/_____

Venue

\

SAMPLE JUDGE'S CONTRACT

This agreement made and entered into this **date** by and between the **Art Association** and **Judges Name** (hereinafter "Judge").

Art Association is desirous of utilizing the professional services of the Judge to officiate at the **Name Of Art Show** to be held on **Date** at **Address** and to judge all classes as outlined in the prospectus included herein.

It is mutually agreed and understood between the Judge and *Art Association* as follows:

For and in consideration of the Judge performing the functions mentioned herein, **agrees** to compensate the Judge for $**Fee** per show day.

Art Association agrees to provide or

reimburse the Judge for lunch expenses.

Automobile travel expenses will be reimbursed from the judge's residence to the show at the rate allowed by the IRS per mile. The judge will turn in a mileage expense sheet to the show chair upon arrival at the show.

The Judge agrees to arrive at the **Address Of The Show** at **Time**.

Judge will bring a sample of his/her art to be shown during the **Show**. The show will run from **Date** to **Date**.

Pick up of art shall be on **Date** at **Time**. The Judge is responsible for picking up his/her art at the close of the show. While every attempt will be made to insure the safety of the art, the **Art Association** or the **Show** venue assumes no responsibility for loss or damage to the art for any reason whatsoever.

Show Chairman, *Art Association Name*

Ju

dge

APPROVED

_____

_____

_____

_____

Address_____

City, State,
        Zip_____

_____

Phone – including area code

_____

_____

Email _____

SAMPLE SHOW PROFIT &

LOSS STATEMENT

Approximate Show Profit/Loss

Expenses	
Gallery Rental using our standards	$200.00
Judge	$100.00
Awards based on 6 categories	
Best of Show	$150.00
1st Places - $50 ea.	$300.00
2nd Places - $25 ea.	$150.00
3rd Places - $15 ea.	$90.00
Advertising	$0.00
Ribbons	$0.00
Printing	$0.00
Prospectus	$12.00
show catalog	$12.00
Art Cards	$10.00
Total Expenses=	**$1,024.00**

Income	
Entry Fees	
No of Entries Needed to break even	
Actual Entries	**Total fees**
Entry Fees @ $22 each Non-Member	47
	$1,024.00
Entry Fees @ 30 each Non-Member	$660.00
Entry fees @ $20- each Member	60
	$1,204.71
Grants & Gifts	$0.00
Total Income	**$236.00**

CHECK LIST FOR SHOWS

Date				Amount needed	Time/Date	Handled?
Show Hours						
Location						
	Parking					
Entry Fees						
	Members					
	Non Members					
Time						
Judging						
	Volunteers to assist: runners, note takers					
Receiving						
	How many volunteers					
		Rules to give volunteers				
	Date & Time					
Set Up Show						
	Design for display					
	Standards					
	Hanging Art					
	Volunteers					
	Decoration					
Reception						
	Set Up					
	Food					
	Plates, silverware, napkins, tablecloths, etc.					
	Clean Up					
Take Down Show						
	Volunteers					
Misc. Issues						
	How many judges?					
		Rules to give judges				
		Rules to give helpers				

PROMOTION FEE EXPENSE

CHART

Promotion Type	Promotion Date	Cost	Gallery to Pay %50	Artist to Pay %50
ADVERTISING POSTERS				
RADIO SPOT				
TV SPOT				
HANDOUTS				
FOOD FOR RECEPTION				
TABLE/CHAIR RENTS				
CATERER				

VENUE/GALLERY

COMMISSION LIST

If you are displaying in an unconventional venue such as a coffee shop, restaurant or other retail venue, it may be that the venue will be willing to sell the art for you. In that case, you will need to add the following list to your venue contract.

Art No	Title	Medium	Size	Retail Price	Gallery/Venue Commission	Your Net Income
1						
2						
3						
4						
5						
6						
7						
8						
9						
10						
11						
12						
13						
14						
15						
16						
17						
18						
19						
20						
21						

ABOUT THE AUTHOR

Gail Daley is a self-taught artist and writer with a background in business. An omnivorous reader, she was inspired by her son, also a writer, to finish some of the incomplete novels she had begun over the years. She is heavily involved in local art groups and fills her time reading, writing, painting in acrylics, and spending time with her husband of 40 plus years. Currently her family is owned by two cats, a mischievous young cat called Mab (after the fairy queen of air and darkness) and a mellow Gray Princess named Moonstone. In the past, the family shared their home with many dogs, cats and a Guinea Pig, all of whom have passed over the rainbow bridge. A recent major surgery on her stomach and a bout with breast cancer has slowed her down a little, but she continues to write and paint.

GAIL'S OTHER BOOKS

NON-FICTION
The Complete Modern Artist's Handbook
PAMPHLETS
Introduction To The Internet #1
The Hard Stuff – Handbook #2
Art Show Basics – Handbook #3
Framing on a Budget – Handbook #4
Making Money At Arts & Craft Shows –
Handbook #5
FICTION

THE HANDFASTING SERIES
A Year & A Day
Forever & A Day
All Our Tomorrows
From This Day Forward
To Love & Honor
Uncharted Trails
For Now & Always (ETA* Fall 2019)
THE PORTAL WORLD TALES
ST. ANTONI SERIES
Warriors of St. Antoni
The Enforcers (ETA* Spring 2020)
MAGI SERIES
Spell Of The Magi
Magi Storm (ETA* Fall 2018)

NOTES